QUICKREADS

LEVEL A • BOOK 3

Elfrieda H. Hiebert, Ph.D.

SAVVAS
LEARNING COMPANY

Program Reviewers and Consultants

Dr. Barbara A. Baird
Director of Federal Programs/Richardson ISD
Richardson, TX

Dr. Kate Kinsella
Dept. of Secondary Education and Step to College Program
San Francisco State University
San Francisco, CA

Pat Sears
Early Childhood Coordinator/Virginia Beach Public Schools
Virginia Beach, VA

Dr. Judith B. Smith
Supervisor of ESOL and World and Classical Languages/Baltimore City Public Schools
Baltimore, MD

Savvas Learning Company LLC, 15 East Midland Avenue, Paramus, NJ 07652

SAVVAS
LEARNING COMPANY

ISBN-13: 978-1-4284-3149-2
ISBN-10: 1-4284-3149-7
19 22

CONTENTS

CONTENTS

SCIENCE

Floating and Sinking

CONTENTS

SOCIAL STUDIES

Toys of Long Ago

SOCIAL STUDIES

American Stories

CONTENTS

Acknowledgments

Photographs

Photo locators denoted as follows: Top (T), Center (C), Bottom (B), Left (L), Right (R), Background (Bkgd)

Cover: ©moodboard/SuperStock; **3** Digital Vision/Getty Images; **4** ©Margoe Edwards/Shutterstock; **5** Shutterstock; **6** Pixland/Thinkstock; **7** ©StampGirl/Shutterstock; **8** ©Marion Bull/Alamy; **10** Digital Vision/Getty Images; **12** ©Fancy/Alamy; **14** Agnieszka Kirinicjanow/Getty Images; **16** ©Sergey Lavrentev/Shutterstock; **18** ©Rob Byron/Shutterstock; **24** ©Padmayogini/Shutterstock; **26** Creatas images/Thinkstock; **28** ©Margoe Edwards/Shutterstock; **30** ©ronfromyork/Shutterstock; **32** ©Tischenko Irina/Shutterstock; **38** Goodshoot/Thinkstock; **42** Jupiterimages/Thinkstock; **44** Shutterstock; **46** ©Olga Lyubkina/Shutterstock; **52** Shutterstock; **54** ©Mike Rex/Alamy Images; **56** ©Tony Freeman/PhotoEdit, Inc.; **58** Pixland/Thinkstock; **60** ©Fancy/Alamy; **66** ©Nikreates/Alamy; **68** ©SuperStock/SuperStock; **70** ©Racheal Grazias/Shutterstock; **72** ©StampGirl/Shutterstock; **74** Everett Collection, Inc.; **80** ©Marion Bull/Alamy; **82** Richard Hook/©DK Images; **84** David King/ Courtesy of The Museum of London/DK Images; **86** Digital Vision/Getty Images; **88** Christopher and Sally Gable/©DK Images.

Science on the Playground

A playground is a good place to both learn and play.

Playground Scientists

A playground is a great place to learn about science. People who study science learn about how things work. When children ask questions about why one ball bounces higher than another, they are being scientists.

Scientists look for answers to their questions by studying things and by keeping track of what they find. Playground scientists might try balls of different sizes to see how high they bounce. Playground scientists might also try balls that are made of different things to see how high they bounce. Games on playgrounds can be even more fun when children know how things work.

Science on the Playground

Knowing about science can help people run faster.

Running Races

Many children run races on playgrounds. Knowing about science can help children pick the places on the playground where they can run fastest.

Some playgrounds have two parts, with sand on one part and blacktop on the other part. A race on sand makes a runner's feet work hard. Because sand is soft, the ground moves a little when a foot hits it. The moving ground slows a runner down.

On the other hand, blacktop does not move. A runner's foot lifts off blacktop faster than it lifts off sand. This means that runners can run faster on blacktop than on sand.

Science on the Playground

In kickball, players can kick the ball or run with it.

Kickball

Kickball is like baseball, but players don't use a bat. Players on two teams take turns kicking a ball and running around bases. Players who kick the ball far get around more bases and win the game.

Players can use what they know about science to make kickball hard or easy to play. Small, heavy balls can go very far. However, small, heavy balls can be hard to kick. Balls that are big and don't weigh much can be easy to kick. However, these balls won't go far. The best balls for kickball are not too big and not too hard.

Science on the Playground

The riders on seesaws take turns going up and down.

Seesaws

A seesaw is a board that is balanced on a low fence. One person sits on each end of the board, and the riders take turns going up and down. The ride goes on until the riders stop pushing off from the ground.

Science helps seesaw riders who don't weigh the same. This is because a seesaw has to be balanced. To balance a seesaw, the heavier person has to sit closer to the center of the board. However, the heavier person has to sit far enough away from the center so that his feet touch the ground when the seesaw is down.

Science on the Playground

Pushing harder makes a swing go higher and higher.

Swings

How do swings work? As a person starts to swing, the seat moves along the curve of a circle. As the person pushes harder and the swing goes higher, the seat moves through a longer curve of the circle.

A person who swings high seems to have a longer ride, but this is not so. One swing ride takes as long as any other swing ride. No matter how high a person goes, the time of the swing ride is the same.

Become a scientist and test this when you are on a playground. All you need is a watch and a swing!

Review Science on the Playground

Write words that will help you remember what you learned.

Playground Scientists

Running Races

Kickball

Seesaws

Swings

Playground Scientists

1. "Playground Scientists" is MAINLY about how to ____

Ⓐ make up games on playgrounds.
Ⓑ ask questions about ball games.
Ⓒ learn about science on playgrounds.

2. How do scientists find answers to their questions?

____

____

____

Running Races

1. Runners' feet work hard on sand because the ground ____

Ⓐ does not move when their feet hit it.
Ⓑ moves when their feet hit it.
Ⓒ helps runners move their feet very fast.

2. Can runners race faster on sand or on blacktop? Why?

____

____

____

Review Science on the Playground

Kickball

1. Another good name for "Kickball" is ____

Ⓐ "Science and Kickball."

Ⓑ "Rules for Kickball."

Ⓒ "Making Teams for Kickball."

2. How can science help someone play kickball?

____

____

____

Seesaws

1. Why does a seesaw have to be balanced?

Ⓐ so the riders can go up and down

Ⓑ so the board can turn around

Ⓒ so the riders will weigh the same

2. How does knowing about science help seesaw riders who don't weigh the same?

____

____

____

Swings

1. In what kind of line does a swing move?
   Ⓐ in a circle
   Ⓑ in a flat line
   Ⓒ in a curve

2. How are all swing rides the same?

____

____

____

Connect Your Ideas

1. Tell about two ways you can use science on a playground.

____

____

____

2. Why is it helpful to know how things work on a playground?

____

____

____

Solids, Liquids, and Gases

Everything in this picture is made of matter.

Matter

Everything on Earth is made of something called matter. The air, our hands, and water are all made of matter. Air, hands, and water do not look the same. However, the matter in air, hands, and water is the same.

While all matter is the same, matter can take different forms. Air is matter in the form of gas. Water is matter in liquid form. Hands are matter in solid form.

One form of matter can change into another form. Ice can change into water. Water can change into steam. Steam can change back into water, and water can change into ice.

Solids, Liquids, and Gases

Ice cream is a solid that can become a liquid.

Solids

An ice cube, a book, and a chair are all examples of solid matter. Solids keep their shape, even when they are pushed or pulled. A chair looks the same, no matter how hard it is pushed or pulled. Solid matter also stays the same size, even when it is moved. A book can be moved from a big box to a small box. The book stays the same size even when the size of the box is different.

Solids keep their size and shape. However, some solids, like ice cubes, can change into another form of matter when they are heated.

Solids, Liquids, and Gases

Water takes the shape of the glass it is in.

Liquids

Water and milk are matter in liquid form. Liquids take the shape of whatever they are in. If water is in a cup, it takes the shape of the cup. If water is in a vase, it takes the shape of the vase. Without a cup or vase, water spills and spreads.

Liquids stay the same size even when they are moved. If water is moved from a large cup to a small cup, there is no less water. If the cup is too small, the water spills over. Like solid matter, liquid matter can change into another form when it is heated.

Solids, Liquids, and Gases

Gas can take the shape of any balloon.

Gases

Both the air around us and the air in balloons are matter in gas form. Like liquids, gases take the shape of whatever they are in. The air in a heart-shaped balloon takes the shape of the heart. The air in a ball takes the shape of the ball.

Gases also fill space. If gas is moved from a small ball to a large ball, it fills the space in the large ball.

Like some solids and liquids, some gases change into another form of matter when they are cooled. Steam is a gas that turns into water when it is cooled.

Solids, Liquids, and Gases

What forms of matter do you see in this picture?

Mixing Forms of Matter

Different forms of matter can often be found close to each other or even mixed together. For example, a cup of hot tea has a solid, a liquid, and a gas near each other. The cup is the solid, the tea is the liquid, and the steam coming off the tea is the gas.

A fizzy soda with ice cubes has a solid, a liquid, and a gas mixed together. The ice cubes are solids. The soda is the liquid, and the fizz is the gas. Everything on Earth is one of these three forms of matter.

Review Solids, Liquids, and Gases

Write words that will help you remember what you learned.

Matter

Solids

Liquids

Gases

Mixing Forms of Matter

Matter

1. How are the air, hands, and water the same?
   Ⓐ All can be found in three forms.
   Ⓑ All are made of matter.
   Ⓒ All are made of solids and liquids.

2. Tell about two forms that water can take.

____

____

____

Solids

1. What are three examples of solid matter?
   Ⓐ ice cubes, books, and chairs
   Ⓑ air, ice cubes, and people
   Ⓒ hands, dogs, and water

2. How are all solids alike?

____

____

____

Review Solids, Liquids, and Gases

Liquids

1. What are two examples of liquid matter?

Ⓐ ice and water

Ⓑ water and milk

Ⓒ air and water

2. How are all liquids alike?

Gases

1. What happens when gas is moved from one place to another?

Ⓐ The gas takes the shape of water.

Ⓑ The gas changes into another form.

Ⓒ The gas fills the place it is in.

2. How are all gases alike?

Mixing Forms of Matter

1. Solids, liquids, and gases are forms of matter that ____

Ⓐ can never be mixed together.

Ⓑ can be found close to each other.

Ⓒ can all take the shape of whatever they are in.

2. What are the three forms of matter in a fizzy soda?

____

____

____

Connect Your Ideas

1. Tell how two of the three kinds of matter are alike.

____

____

____

2. Tell how two of the three kinds of matter are different.

____

____

____

Floating and Sinking

What things do you know that float on water?

What Floats?

If a nail falls into a tub of water, it falls to the bottom of the tub. When this happens, we say that the nail sinks in water. If a block of wood falls into the same tub, the wood stays on top of the water. We say that the block of wood floats on water.

Some things, like nails, rocks, and sand, sink in water. Other things, like blocks of wood and pieces of paper, float on water. Knowing why things sink or float helps people build ships and other things that will be used in water.

Floating and Sinking

A block of wood will float, but rocks will sink in water.

Will It Float or Sink?

When a block of wood floats, most of the block is above water. Only a small part is under water. This small part of the block has pushed away, or displaced, some water. When water is displaced, something has taken its place. We say that the block has displaced the water.

If the object weighs the same as the water that has been displaced, the object floats. This is why a block of wood floats. If the object weighs more than the water that has been displaced, the object sinks. This is why a rock sinks.

Floating and Sinking

A ship's bottom is shaped to let it displace water.

Why Ships Float

It may seem that all light things should float and all heavy things should sink, but this is not so. Steel ships are big and heavy, but they can move across the ocean. Why do ships float?

A block of steel will sink in water. However, a ship's bottom is not shaped like a block. Instead, a ship's bottom is shaped in a way that lets it displace water. If a ship has a hole, though, its bottom will no longer displace water. Instead, the hole will let water come into the ship, and the ship will sink.

Floating and Sinking

This swimmer is using air in tanks so she can stay under water.

Swimming and Air

How do fish move back and forth from the bottom of the ocean to the ocean's surface? Most fish have airbags called swim bladders. When their airbags are full of air, fish float up to the ocean's surface. When their airbags are empty, though, fish drop down to the ocean's bottom.

People's lungs work like the swim bladders of fish. When swimmers take long, deep breaths, their lungs fill with air. The air helps swimmers float at the surface of the pool. When their lungs are empty, though, swimmers drop down to the bottom of the pool.

Floating and Sinking

Life jackets help people float on water.

Life Jackets

Life jackets can keep people safe in and around water. Wearing a life jacket is like having lungs on the outside of the body. Unlike the lungs inside the body, however, a life jacket is always full of air.

When people wear life jackets, they displace, or push away, enough water to keep floating. Even when their lungs are empty, people who are wearing life jackets will keep floating.

Some swimming suits for young children now have life jackets built into them. These swimming suits can help young children keep floating even when they don't take long, deep breaths.

Review Floating and Sinking

Write words that will help you remember what you learned.

What Floats?

____

____

____

____

Will It Float or Sink?

____

____

____

____

Why Ships Float

____

____

____

____

Swimming and Air

____

____

____

____

Life Jackets

____

____

____

____

What Floats?

1. "What Floats?" is MAINLY about ____

Ⓐ why things float or sink.

Ⓑ what things float or sink.

Ⓒ how to make wood float.

2. Why might a person need to know what floats on water?

____

____

____

Will It Float or Sink?

1. When water is displaced, something ____

Ⓐ floats on a block of wood.

Ⓑ weighs more than a rock.

Ⓒ takes its place.

2. Why do rocks sink in water?

____

____

____

Review Floating and Sinking

Why Ships Float

1. What could make a ship sink?

Ⓐ displacing the water around it
Ⓑ making the ship from steel
Ⓒ having a hole in the bottom

2. Why do ships float?

____

____

____

Swimming and Air

1. What part of a fish's body helps it float and sink?

Ⓐ the air around its fins
Ⓑ the water in its lungs
Ⓒ its swim bladders

2. How are people's lungs like the swim bladders of fish?

____

____

____

Life Jackets

1. How are life jackets like people's lungs?
Ⓐ The air in them helps people float.
Ⓑ The water in them helps people sink.
Ⓒ They are on the outside of the body.

2. How do life jackets work?

Connect Your Ideas

1. Choose two things you learned about in these readings. Tell why these things float or sink.

2. Suppose you were going to make something to keep people safe in water. How would it work?

Toys of Long Ago

This doll was made from parts of a corn plant.

How Toys Were Made

Just like the children of today, children of long ago played with toys. Some of the toys of long ago were the same as the toys children use today. However, the toys of long ago were made at home. Sometimes, the children made their own toys. A marble could be made from a ball of clay. A doll could be made from a corn cob.

Clay marbles or dolls made of corn cobs look different from the marbles and dolls of today. However, children of long ago played many of the same games with their toys that children play today.

Toys of Long Ago

These dolls were made long ago.

Dolls

The oldest toy that has been found is a doll. Someone played with this doll thousands of years ago. It would have been hard to hug the doll because it was made of wood. Until not long ago, dolls were made of materials like wood, cloth, wool, or even plants. Dolls were made at home, not bought in stores.

Today, many kinds of dolls can be bought in stores. These dolls are made of material that lets children move the dolls' arms, legs, and head. Some dolls even seem to talk. Best of all, many dolls today are soft and easy to hug.

This yo-yo trick is called "cat's cradle."

Yo-Yos

Even thousands of years ago, children played with yo-yos. Early yo-yos could only go up and down. Today's yo-yos, however, can spin, too.

It takes skill to learn yo-yo tricks like "walking the dog" and "around the world." The trick called "walking the dog" is done when someone gets the yo-yo to spin fast as it moves along the floor. The trick called "around the world" is done when someone spins a yo-yo around in the air.

In 1985, a yo-yo was taken on a spaceship. Pictures of yo-yo tricks done in the spaceship showed people how things work in space.

Toys of Long Ago

These children are flying a kite on a beach.

Kites

Kites are another toy that children have used for many years. Early kites were made of many different materials. Some of these materials were paper, leaves, and parts of bamboo plants. Bamboo is strong, so bamboo kites won't break in the wind. Bamboo is also light, so bamboo kites can fly easily. Some early kites were even made to look like birds.

Today, kites come in many different sizes and shapes. Because they are made of materials that are even stronger and lighter than bamboo, huge kites can be built. Some are strong enough for someone to sit in and fly.

Toys of Long Ago

This boy is showing how to bounce marbles off of one another.

Marbles

Marbles have been found that are more than one thousand years old. These marbles of long ago were often made of clay, stone, or even nuts. Today, most marbles are made of glass.

Marbles of long ago were made in different sizes and had different patterns. Today's marbles also are made in different sizes and have different patterns. The patterns of today's glass marbles can be so different that adults buy them, too.

Pictures from long ago show children playing marble games. These games look much like today's marble games. However, children and even adults today make up new games with marbles, too.

Review Toys of Long Ago

Write words that will help you remember what you learned.

How Toys Were Made

____

____

____

____

Dolls

____

____

____

____

Yo-Yos

____

____

____

____

Kites

____

____

____

____

Marbles

____

____

____

____

How Toys Were Made

1. The toys of long ago were made ____
   Ⓐ in stores.
   Ⓑ at home.
   Ⓒ by teachers.

2. What is one way children made toys long ago?

____

____

____

Dolls

1. "Dolls" is MAINLY about ____
   Ⓐ the world's oldest dolls.
   Ⓑ how to make dolls.
   Ⓒ dolls from long ago and today.

2. Tell about two ways dolls today are different from dolls of long ago.

____

____

____

Review Toys of Long Ago

Yo-Yos

1. Using a yo-yo in space showed people ____
   Ⓐ how things work in space.
   Ⓑ how spaceships work.
   Ⓒ how to make up new tricks for yo-yos.

2. Tell about one of the yo-yo tricks in this reading.

____

____

____

Kites

1. Some early kites were made of bamboo because ____
   Ⓐ people did not have any other materials.
   Ⓑ bamboo is strong and light.
   Ⓒ bamboo could be made to look like a bird.

2. How are today's kites different from early kites?

____

____

____

Marbles

1. How are marbles today different from marbles of long ago?
   Ⓐ Marbles today are all the same size.
   Ⓑ Marbles today have patterns.
   Ⓒ Marbles today are made of glass.

2. Name two materials that were used to make marbles long ago.

____

____

____

Connect Your Ideas

1. How are two toys today different from the way they were long ago?

____

____

____

2. How are two toys today like the way they were long ago?

____

____

____

American Stories

The first flag had one star and one stripe for each of the first 13 states.

The Stars and Stripes

George Washington led the army in the war to make the United States a country. Before the United States became a country, many states had their own flag.

George Washington thought that the army needed to have one flag. One flag would show that the United States was one country. The new flag had one star for each state. It also had one stripe for each of the first 13 states. The stars and stripes made this new flag different from any other country's flag. Once the army used it, everyone began using the new American flag.

American Stories

In this picture, the British are trying to stop Paul Revere on his ride.

The Ride

The war had begun. The British were going to Concord to stop the Americans from forming their own country. Paul Revere and Billy Dawes had to warn the people of Concord that the British were coming. Late at night, Paul Revere and Billy Dawes started their ride to Concord. Along the way, they warned many people to get ready for the British army.

Before Paul Revere and Billy Dawes could get to Concord, the British stopped them. However, someone else took their news to Concord. The next day, when the British got to Concord, the Americans were ready for them.

Many people visit Philadelphia every year to see the Liberty Bell.

The Liberty Bell

In Philadelphia, the Liberty Bell rings every year to mark our country's birthday. The bell was made in 1751. Philadelphia wrote its laws in 1701, so the bell marked the 50th birthday of those laws.

The Liberty Bell cracked the first time it was rung. Although it was fixed several times, the bell still had a crack. It was rung in 1776 when the United States was founded. Ever since 1839, it has been called the Liberty Bell.

The Liberty Bell is still cracked and is now only tapped, not rung. However, the bell makes us think about what it means to be free.

American Stories

This stamp shows a picture of Uncle Sam.

"Uncle Sam"

"Uncle Sam" is one nickname for the United States. This nickname came from a man named Sam Wilson, whom many people called "Uncle Sam."

The Americans and the British were fighting during the War of 1812. At that time, Sam Wilson sold meat to the American army. He put "U.S." on the meat. He meant this to stand for the "United States." However, people joked that "U.S." really meant "Uncle Sam."

Soon, people who didn't even know Sam Wilson joked that things from the U.S. came from Uncle Sam. That is how "Uncle Sam" became a nickname for the United States.

American Stories

This painting shows Francis Scott Key on a ship, looking at the American flag.

"The Star-Spangled Banner"

"The Star-Spangled Banner" is our country's song. Francis Scott Key wrote the song's words during the War of 1812. This war was between the British and the Americans.

During one fight, Francis Scott Key went onto a British ship to help free a friend. The British kept the men on the ship until the next day.

In the morning, Francis Scott Key saw the American flag flying. America had won the fight! Francis Scott Key was so happy that he wrote "The Star-Spangled Banner." He wrote that America was "the land of the free and the home of the brave."

Review American Stories

Write words that will help you remember what you learned.

The Stars and Stripes

____

____

____

____

The Ride

____

____

____

____

The Liberty Bell

____

____

____

____

"Uncle Sam"

____

____

____

____

"The Star-Spangled Banner"

____

____

____

____

The Stars and Stripes

1. Another good name for "The Stars and Stripes" is ____

Ⓐ "Thirteen Flags."

Ⓑ "America's Flag."

Ⓒ "Washington's Army."

2. Why did George Washington want the United States to have one flag?

____

____

The Ride

1. Paul Revere and Billy Dawes wanted to warn the Americans that ____

Ⓐ the war had begun.

Ⓑ the American army was coming.

Ⓒ the British army was coming.

2. What happened when the British got to Concord?

____

____

____

Review American Stories

The Liberty Bell

1. Why is the Liberty Bell rung every year?

Ⓐ to tell the time in Philadelphia

Ⓑ to mark the day that Philadelphia was founded

Ⓒ to mark the birthday of the United States

2. What does the Liberty Bell make Americans think about?

___

___

___

"Uncle Sam"

1. "Uncle Sam" is a nickname for ____

Ⓐ someone in the American army.

Ⓑ the United States.

Ⓒ meat that was sold to the Americans.

2. Tell how the United States got the nickname "Uncle Sam."

___

___

___

"The Star-Spangled Banner"

1. "The Star-Spangled Banner" is MAINLY about ____

Ⓐ writing songs.

Ⓑ wars in America.

Ⓒ our country's song.

2. Why did Francis Scott Key write "The Star-Spangled Banner"?

____

____

____

Connect Your Ideas

1. What are two American stories you read about?

____

____

____

2. Suppose there was another reading. Do you think it would be about George Washington or the songs of today? Why?

____

____

____

The Stone Age

Scientists study art, tools, and bones to learn about the people of long ago.

The Earliest People

While people have been on Earth for a long time, not much is known about the earliest people. That is because no one has found any art or tools that the earliest people may have made. Studying things like bowls or spears can tell scientists how people lived long ago.

Once people learned to make tools, they made drawings on the walls of caves. They also made bowls and spears. The earliest tools that have been found were made from stones. Because the people from long ago used stones to make tools, scientists have called this time "The Stone Age."

Tools made with stones and sticks helped early people hunt animals.

Tools

The earliest people likely used sticks to get food. Later, people made tools from stones and animal bones. These new tools were stronger and lasted longer than sticks. Stronger tools helped people hunt for animals without getting close to them. People could also catch fish with hooks that they made from animal bones. In this way, tools helped early people get more food and stay safe.

Early people also used stones to make fire. If people rubbed two stones together, the stones made sparks of fire. Fire helped early people stay warm, cook food, and keep wild animals away.

The Stone Age

These tools helped Stone-Age farmers grow food and crush grain.

Food

Early people moved from place to place to hunt animals and find plants to eat. In winter, food was hard to find. However, stone tools helped people dig holes to hide seeds from animals. Once people learned to grow plants, though, they did not have to go looking for food.

Some of the first plants that people grew were grains like corn, wheat, and rice. Then people learned to make flour by using stones to crush and grind grain. They also learned to store flour for winter, when plants did not grow. Growing and storing food helped early people feed themselves all year.

The Stone Age

As they did in the Stone Age, people today use dogs to herd sheep.

Animals

At first, Stone-Age people hunted animals for food. Over time, though, people found that animals could be used in other ways, too. People began to tame the animals that we now call goats, cows, sheep, and dogs. Goats and cows made milk that people used as food. People used the wool from sheep to keep warm. People used dogs to herd other animals, like sheep. Dogs also kept people safe from wild animals.

Once people learned to tame horses, their lives got even better. This is because horses could move people and things in less time and with less work.

The Stone Age

This cave painting shows various Stone-Age animals.

Cave Paintings

Long ago, people also used stones to carve pictures into cave walls. Sometimes Stone-Age people added color to their cave paintings. Over time, the colors in these cave paintings have become less bright. However, scientists can still learn a lot about life in the Stone Age by looking at cave paintings.

Stone-Age people did not have a way of writing. Instead, scientists think that Stone-Age people told stories by painting on the walls of caves. These cave paintings helped people tell about their past. The paintings also showed important things in Stone-Age people's lives.

Review The Stone Age

Write words that will help you remember what you learned.

The Earliest People

Tools

Food

Animals

Cave Paintings

The Earliest People

1. Why don't scientists know much about the earliest people?
Ⓐ Scientists can't read early people's writing.
Ⓑ Scientists haven't found early people's art or tools.
Ⓒ Early people did not talk about how they lived.

2. How did the earliest people use tools?

____

____

____

Tools

1. "Tools" is MAINLY about ____
Ⓐ where people found tools.
Ⓑ how tools helped early people.
Ⓒ why tools were hard to use.

2. How did early people use stones and animal bones to make tools?

____

____

____

Review The Stone Age

Food

1. Why did early people move from place to place?
   Ⓐ to find grains and flour
   Ⓑ to plant seeds
   Ⓒ to find food to eat

2. How did learning to grow plants help early people?

____

____

____

Animals

1. Another good name for "Animals" is ____
   Ⓐ "Taming Horses."
   Ⓑ "Hunting Animals."
   Ⓒ "Animals and People."

2. Tell about how Stone-Age people used two kinds of animals.

____

____

____

Cave Paintings

1. "Cave Paintings" is MAINLY about how Stone-Age people ____

Ⓐ made colors for painting.

Ⓑ made pictures on cave walls.

Ⓒ told scientists about their lives.

2. Why do scientists think Stone-Age people made cave paintings?

Connect Your Ideas

1. Tell about two ways Stone-Age people made their lives better.

2. Tell about two ways life today is different from life in the Stone Age.

Reading Log • Level A • Book 3

	I Read This	New Words I Learned	New Facts I Learned	What Else I Want to Learn About This Subject
Science on the Playground				
Playground Scientists				
Running Races				
Kickball				
Seesaws				
Swings				
Solids, Liquids, and Gases				
Matter				
Solids				
Liquids				
Gases				
Mixing Forms of Matter				
Floating and Sinking				
What Floats?				
Will It Float or Sink?				
Why Ships Float				
Swimming and Air				
Life Jackets				

	I Read This	New Words I Learned	New Facts I Learned	What Else I Want to Learn About This Subject
Toys of Long Ago				
How Toys Were Made				
Dolls				
Yo-Yos				
Kites				
Marbles				
American Stories				
The Stars and Stripes				
The Ride				
The Liberty Bell				
"Uncle Sam"				
"The Star-Spangled Banner"				
The Stone Age				
The Earliest People				
Tools				
Food				
Animals				
Cave Paintings				

Self-Check Graph

Mark your reading rate here.

	Playground Scientists	Running Races	Kickball	Seesaws	Swings	Matter	Solids	Liquids	Gases	Mixing Forms of Matter	What Floats?	Will It Float or Sink?	Why Ships Float	Swimming and Air	Life Jackets	How Toys Were Made	Dolls	Yo-Yos	Kites	Marbles	The Stars and Stripes	The Ride	The Liberty Bell	"Uncle Sam"	"The Star-Spangled Banner"	The Earliest People	Tools	Food	Animals	Cave Paintings
130																														
128																														
126																														
124																														
122																														
120																														
118																														
116																														
114																														
112																														
110																														
108																														
106																														
104																														
102																														
100																														
98																														
96																														
94																														
92																														
90																														
88																														
86																														
84																														
82																														
80																														
78																														
76																														
74																														
72																														
70																														
68																														
66																														
64																														
62																														
60																														
58																														
56																														
54																														
52																														
50																														